I0202682

Silent drops

Silent drops

Words of the Heart

Hélène Avérous

4 Fourth Revolution
www.FourthRevolutionPublishing.com

Fourth Revolution Publishing
23D Charlton lane
Singapore 539690
www.FourthRevolutionPublishing.com
Silent drops
First Edition, 2014
Copyright ©Fourth Revolution Publishing, 2014

Text design by Hélène Avérous
Illustrations © 2014 Hélène Avérous

All rights reserved. No part of this book may be used or
reproduced in any manner whatsoever, except in the case of
brief quotations embodied in critical articles and reviews,
without written permission from the publisher.

Published in Singapore in 2014
First print – printed in Malaysia
ISBN: 978-981-07-9072-1

To my soul friends
who gave birth to this book

To Thích Nhất Hạnh

Each of His words
Keeps on resonating in me
Like the bell ringing
In the far away countryside
Though held in His own hands

I heard Your call
Coming from nowhere
Not knowing
Who You were

You have no name
But I heard You
And the tears of love
Started flowing from those dry eyes

I can't find Your name
You have all
They make my Heart alive

Am still crying
This silent love

Contents

Preface

Throughout the years, life pushed me to let words flow out of my hands, free to be. It started with long sentences, long explanations about what was witnessed. Little by little, the words became lighter and freer to simply be, without any rational explanations behind them but the freedom to let the words dance.

Those last years have been deeply transforming for me and I am deeply thankful to all the people I have met on this path. I have felt hurt, abandoned, betrayed, supported, cared for, embraced and loved by life itself. Every-one who appears in my life brings a reason to dive deeper into the Heart.

The healing happens when the suffering is acknowledged as a part of oneself. I was suffering and the power of words appeared to me as a practical way of letting go of deep rooted emotions. How often the words that came out ended by blessing me while bringing tears to these eyes.

I have been sharing all of them with friends on the internet for many years. Many of you encouraged me to gather them in a book, so here they are.
I would love to mention each one of you who travel with me on this beautiful path that is life but it would require a full book to mention all of your names.

Meanwhile, I would like to deeply thank a few precious soul friends without whom this book wouldn't exist in terms of both content and form.

To Joshua, Belle and Kia, thank you for your light and patience to correct my "French English" with respect to the weird freedom of the words sometimes.

To Sudhir, Vineet, Stephen, Lacrima and Rajesh, thank you for your presence in my life, it gave birth to this book.

And without my husband and our three precious children, I would not be here today, so, Charlotte, Paul, Emile and Jérémie, simply, thank you to be.

Lastly, a few years ago, I was blessed to find out that life was loving and caring for me through any present forms. It was a few months after a trip alone to India where I reached the holy hill of Arunachala that I have been blessed to meet Thích Nhất Hạnh.
His presence, wisdom and peace made me feel so grateful to be here. The first poem is dedicated to Him and was written after this meeting.

Hélène Avérous

*Peace is already present within us
and can be touched at any moment.
Some call it love.*

Foreword

This fine book by Hélène Avérous is indeed a most beautiful and remarkable work of literary art.

This is because it is inspiringly composed deeply, from the intimacy of the Heart of a lady who is a dedicated spiritual aspirant of the highest calibre; and so the book is consequently emotionally very moving and at the same time most profound.

It is a book to treasure and dip into over and over again for poetic inspiration and refreshing spiritual wisdom. She has visited the sacred pilgrimage mountain of Arunachala, home of the Great Sage Sri Bhagavan Ramana Maharshi in Southern India, and is well versed in his teachings. She has also met the saintly Sage Thich Nhat Hahn, and the renowned spiritual teacher Siva Shakti Ma of Tiruvannamalai. Consequently she is very well versed in the Great Non Dual Teachings of the Higher Religions which inspire and illumine her gem like aphorisms. The well chosen different Chapters admirably cover the deep emotions of a devoted pilgrim walking wisely on the sacred inward path towards the Realisation of her Immortal Self.

This makes it a very special and in its way a most unique book. The Chapter Headings speak for themselves, The Friend, Presence, Stillness, Faith,

Compassion-Grace, Joy, Tenderness-Silence, Peace, Stillness, Light-Life-Sacredness, The Dream, Surrender and Aloneness. It is as if every step of the spiritual journey is beautifully and carefully expressed succinctly and poetically.

One can dip into it over and over again and find on any page refreshing words which will light up the sensitive reader's heart. It is indeed an offering from the Soul and a rich cornucopia of deeply experienced spiritual jewels. Most generously Hélène is devoting any proceeds earned from the book to Children's Charities.

I strongly recommend this marvellous book to all those who yearn for veritable spiritual inspiration coming from the innermost heart. The book has a delightful feminine quality which makes it even more appealing to the earnest reader who is sensitive to a woman's love, empathy and tenderness. Hélène is to be congratulated on authoring and compiling such a moving collection of spiritually inspiring poetic epigrams which will lift the heart and soul of any reader who is fortunate to become acquainted with her marvellous book.

Alan Jacobs
President Ramana Maharshi Foundation UK
London 2014

You

The Friend

1

I've been waiting for my friend so long
Climbing up mountains
Running down valleys
But never... did I meet my friend...

I crossed the sky
I flew through oceans
I asked for help
He never came...

I touched the stars
They burnt my wings
I dived into the Moon
And found the Sun
My friend never came

I took a boat
Left it empty
On the sea of Love

And stayed here alone
Free

You – The Friend

2

I crossed oceans and valleys
Flew above mountains and swam in rivers
All this time, desperately searching for your love
I ended in your arms
I had never left home

3

Each drop of You
Is a diamond pearl
Shining in my Heart

4

Take my hand
We will walk
We've been walking for so long
But please, take my hand
We will keep on walking
Among tears and laughter
Joys and sorrows

We will walk
And hold Silence

5

I have a Friend
Who is silent
Not this silent "missing"
But this silent Presence

And each time
I become Silence
I find Him
In His infinite tenderness

His Presence is so deep
That nobody
Can ever touch It
Or ever know Him

This Friend
Is nobody here
But sings a song for me every morning
Makes the rain fall when I need to cry
Sends me a child when I feel to hug

And still,
Patiently waits for the moment
I come back here

6

I remember from You
What I don't know from me

7

You show me the light
Of this deep Silence
This gives life to love

Namaste my Friend

8

A deep Silence
Between tender words
I meet You here

9

My only Friend
Is the One
Of this moment

10

Love has your name today
The one who hurts
And suffers out loud

Love has your name today
The one who cares
And gives time to his beloved

Love has your name today
The one absent
In the loneliness of time

Love has your name today
The one happy
Who dances with me

Love has your name today
The Secret One
The One who knows
And never
Runs away

11

O Friend of the night!
In Your glorious brilliance
You shine
Through my Heart!

12

Stay with me under that tree
My Beloved
Our fragrance
Will be the One

13

I've been sunk so deeply in You
That it dissolved
The desire of meeting you
One day

14

Sometimes
One just needs
To spend this moment
With a friend
Light
And free

15

Outside the window
There is a tree
That tells me who you are

Like my friend
There is not a single time
I see this tree
When I forget who you are

This tree
Is my friend
Birds and butterflies
Come to see this humble you
For the joy of my heart

16

I let you go
And you come back
In thousands of ways
Oh!
Such a Presence...
I can only tell you
Such a Presence...

17

My only Teacher is the silent One
He has never ever seen
Anything to change in me

Pure Presence
In His deepest Absence
He holds me tight in His arms
When I need to breathe again

He knows He is the white butterfly
I dance with everyday
On the path to now

18

Your
Words
Are
Droplets
Of Ocean
In the sea
Of my Heart

19

If I say
You are beautiful
It is more like
You are beautiful in me
I am beautiful in You

20

I see You

Delicate
As the bud
Freshly bloomed
In the dew

Strong as the immense stillness
Of the Mountain

Any single thought
Can leave You dead
Here

No thought
Can remove
What You are

There is no way to touch You
Your Silence
Is life flowing in Me

21

If You know
I love You
Then
There is no more place
For me to be
I am free

22

Because He knew
That stillness was You
The flowers are blossoming
In Silence
In Your garden

23

You are this Presence
That makes me disappear
Like the color in a white cloud

You are that strength
That makes me realize
The softness of my delicate skin

You are that Faith
That makes me know
The depth of the blue ocean

You are that Silence
That makes me hear
The Heart beating in the blooming mud

24

O Beloved One!

I could tell You the sky is always blue
Or clouds never cry

I could tell You the sun always shines
Or the Heart is just within

I could tell You that the whole world enjoys the dance
Or pretend kind people never harm

I could tell You flowers always smell
Or the grass is always green

But I would lie to You

The only thing that I can do
Is to tell You
I am with You

25

Between You and I
How can one break the link?
There is no link!
Just that empty immense endless space!
And the deep knowing that time is only a question of
form

There is no wish to make

26

Oh my Lord!
I only speak to You
If You are me
Those words are so tender
I must be Love

27

If love is a river
I will hide myself in the clouds
Knowing that one day
My tears will become
Your blood

28

I spend hours
Talking with you
Thinking you exist
But I must surrender
To the truth
That I am only
Talking with mySelf

29

How could there be any future with You?
I disappear
Each time
I am with You

30

You are the wind
I am the dead leaf

You carry me home
Emptiness of the sound

31

You are the one
Watching the leaves falling through me!
And I smile at me
Still searching for You!

32

Sometimes
Even the river
Doesn't sing
Nor does the horizon exist

It is where
I am You

33

How can I ever be separated from You ?
You are the One that I call in despair
You are the One that I laugh with in Joy

In the Space between
You are so deeply me
That I am You

34

There is a love letter
Planted in my Heart

Its Beauty is the fragrance
Of the moment
I meet You

I haven't opened it yet
This is now the gift I offer You
Blindly

35

The sea is my sky
Your breath
My life

36

This intimacy
Is not about you and me

It is all about
Spring in autumn
White in Colors
Day in Night
Joy in Sorrow
Light in Love
Life in Death
Destruction in Creation
Strength in Weakness
Presence in Absence

In the Space
Of this moment
There is an insulting intimacy
You in I

37

In times of loneliness
Just know
That I am here
That's how I love you

Compassion

Grace

38

I see some rain of tears
Falling from the sky
And I do wonder
Who is crying so heavily?

39

A dew pearl of your tears
Touched my Heart
And has transformed
Into a sea of love

40

Huge stream of compassion
Flowing
Strongly melting
Into a deeply tender
Silence of the Heart

41

A wave of tenderness
Coming from that place
Where the little girl
Is held in the arms of the Mother

And the Mother whispering to her
"I love you
Don't be scared
I'll always be here for you"

The little girl started to cry
At last

42

The tears of my soul are ringing
I don't know who is singing that song
Emptiness of the moment
I have disappeared
In your sharp pain

43

I see your suffering
My gift for You
Is to be here
Until you disappear

There is no way
To disappear
But to be here

44

I miss You
And when I realize
You miss me
I become You
Where only love remains

45

In your tears
I see my own sorrow
I hear my own prayer
I feel my own blessing

You are me today
I was you yesterday
Tears will be mine tomorrow

Tears of Grace
Tears of Grace

I am That

46

Such Innocence in the adult
Thinking that Innocence
Is in the child

47

The Being is hurting the one who ignores
He is It

48

Take my hand
And all those thoughts
Will fly away

In this search of a pure Heart
I see suffering
And the fear of creating suffering

In this moment
I choose to live
As if I was already free

Just take my hand
And all those thoughts
Will fly away

49

Through her fragrance
She called me from far away
I saw her
She caught my breath

50

If He alone had to give You
A single name
Grace would be yours

51

I always have those tears just about to fall
Not knowing why

As if the world was in those tears
Just about to fall

And all that
In a flow of deep peace
Because I know you are here

52

When She silently entered the room
I started to cry immediately
I couldn't stop hearing those words in my mind
"She is so beautiful
She is so beautiful
Just Grace
Grace
Grace"

When I came into Her room
I just fell in tears before being able to look
Into Her eyes
Bowing down at Her feet

Then I looked up and dived into Her eyes
She's been silent for so long
I could hear the dialogue
Between my heart and Hers
Me, desperately yelling in Silence
"We are God, aren't we?"

And Her answer was a huge
"Yes, You are!
You are so beautiful
You are so much loved!"

Compassion ~ Grace

I saw the sparkles of endless love in Her eyes
I knew I had been blessed by Grace

Those words were written in
Tiruvannamalai, India in
2011, after having met Siva
Shakti Ma, a silent one.

53

Namaste to the One
Who takes this hand
Not because it is good to take a desperate hand

Namaste to the One
Who knows there is no hand to take
But the Heart to touch

Namaste to the One
Who sees no difference
In the mist or under the sunny sky

Namaste to the One
Who keeps on being wholeheartedly present
In that moment

54

What is sacred for You
Is sacred for me
Because You are sacred

55

You just let me be
And if it is only for That
Thank you for being

In Your Silence
Between your seldom words
I am so clearly
MySelf

56

I am under Your Grace
Please, let me stay here
For a moment

Don't take anything personally
Let me be under Your Grace

Please, let me see You as the Beloved
So I can stay under Your Grace

Just for a moment
Please, let yourself be
The eternal Beloved

57

When you are sad or lost in sorrow
Love yourself
All the tenderness you're looking for, is within

When the anger is taking over you,
Love yourself
All the forgiveness you require is within

When you don't like someone,
Love yourself
All the wisdom you need is within

When you don't feel love
Love yourself
All the love you miss is within

When you are in despair
Love yourself
All the compassion you claim is within

When there is no one who can help you
Love yourself
The only friend you have is within

When you need tenderness
Love yourself
All the sweetness you deserve is within

When the day is hard to go through
Love yourself
All the softness of one's heart is within

When life disappoints you
Love yourself
Faith is within

When you feel lonely
Love yourself
He is always with you

When you are happy
Love yourself
You deserve that

When you love yourself
There is nobody else to love

58

Oh no, I wouldn't change my wet eyes
With the dryness of the mind
Life is made of tears and laughter
Now my eyes are raining
And I can't know
If it ever comes from anything
Called sadness or joy
Love overflowing
I am alive
Water's running

Gratitude

59

See my tears
Through the eyes of love
And you will see Grace flowing

Joy

60

Drink love
As if this moment
Was the only drop of light
You'll ever have

This thirst
Is what makes your wings flap
In a joyful sound
Of pure happiness

All your life is contained
In that single drop of water

61

The spontaneous truth of the child
Is pure like a clear sky in summer

62

I was kissed by the sky this morning
And noticed
The birds kept on singing

Joy

63

When the music is over
It will be too late to dance!

64

Let the colors
Sing their song!

65

Barefoot
Kiss the sun with your feet

And make the sky
Bloom into colors

66

Let the music sing
The song of your heart!

67

There is a bird singing in my heart
Please, let him be!

There is a bird singing in my heart
That is just for me!

There is bird singing in my heart
Please, let me be!

68

Put a flower in your heart
And paint diamonds in the sky!

69

Fly Beloved!
Live Your life!
Spread your wings
Tear up Your Heart
And sing!

Pierce the sky
And let release
All those secret notes
Captured by Grace
In Your Being

Fly Beloved!
Live Your Life!
Spread Your wings!
Love will make You
Come back to me!

70

What about dancing with words?
Stopping giving them a meaning?
Just the dance of sounds
Echoing in the Heart
Without any meaning

The silent song of words
Whirling through the Being
And dancing
Pure life of no words

71

Be free like a bird
And sing a joyful song
For an endless sky

72

Put your heart in a gift
No matter who
You offer it to

Put your heart in a gift
This gift is your heart

No expectation
No attachment

Just
Put your heart in a gift
And be happy!

73

Don't try to catch the wind
You'll be exhausted

Be the leaf flying joyfully
Carried by its breath
You'll become the wind

74

It is always the last Dance
There will be no other moment
To dance
But now

75

There is a love song
Just on my lips
It is a silent one

There is a love song
Right in my heart
The birds are singing it for you

There is a love song
This is the one
You are singing
For me

76

And suddenly, I realized
That each of my steps
Was making the world turn round
Under my feet

77

Listen to the sound
Of the blown out candle

It tells you
About Joy and Life

78

Inner sparkles
Dance happily
Smiling at the known
Free of being
Pure Joy

79

I am dancing in the night!
I am totally drunk by that dance!

Lost in that non feeling
Intoxicated by the darkness of the unknown Soul
Dancing in itSelf

I am dancing in the night!
Drums are playing the music of the Spirit
There is no-one to dance that dance with me

I am dancing in the night!
I must drink that wine
That makes me forget
All that love I have not realized yet!

I am totally drunk
By the dance itself

I am lost in the Sky
Nobody can see me

I am lost in the Sky

80

Rain is singing
Its soft melody
Roofs are drumming
Leaves are dancing
Flowers are giggling

81

I woke up this morning
And saw
That the sky had bloomed

82

Left here
In a kiss

83

I will dance until you catch me dead...

84

Where only dance remains
I am free
Alone
With or without you
Just dance

A hymn singing
Through the heart beats
Leads the rhythm of the moment

Just the dance
Shining itself
Sometimes in a desperate last surrender to you
Sometimes in the agony of death
Sometimes in the tenderness of the new-born
Sometimes in the longing of the stars

This rhythm...
Cycle of life...
Dance itself

And the melody
Plays a song
In the Heart
Of the lover

Joy

The rhythm
Slows down
And down
Disappears
Held
By...

Silence

But the dance is not over!
Waves of sparkling beings!
Shining in the darkest night
Light the fire of love!

Fireworks of beings
Makes this dream alive!

The Heart!
The Heart is alive!

85

When you really smile
Not only your face is smiling
But your whole world

86

This is life!
Joy, tears, laughter, worries, sharing, giving, receiving

All in wonder!
Life is happening!
The flow happens
And is Life!

Yes, one dies at any moment
And one disappears
In the same time
Life lives itself

Witness of that
There is Joy!
There is Joy!
Sheer Joy!

Tenderness

87

Such a softness in those tears
Like a silent melody
Reaching that place
Where tenderness
Kisses your forehead
With a blissful peace

Some say it is raining here
I see
Only the sky
Crying for me

88

Whatever appears to be outside
There is an infinite
Source of Tenderness
And Peace
Within

89

Stop crying little bird!
Or love your tears!
You will fly tomorrow
Now it is time to rest
In the hands
Of your Beloved

90

Immense tenderness of the rose
The touch of the soft petal
Is melting with its endless intoxicating scent

You are that flower of immense tenderness
And the flower doesn't need to be cut
To be alive in the Heart

Let the flower live
Its own life of Grace
And release its fragrance until no death

91

I fell into a well of tenderness
Whose name is yours
Walls are rose petals flying

That endless fall
Meets the sky
Under my skin

92

This well of Tenderness
Embraces
And dissolves all
That appears to be

Let it be
And lightly burn
Past, present, future
It is pure Compassion
Strength and Light

Embracing all
With the same
Infinite transparent love
In a deep Silence

93

There
Is
Never
Ever
Enough
Tenderness
To be
Bathed
In

94

Love said to me
May your night
Be embraced
By tenderness

95

This blessing flower
Is an offering
Of the Self

As a moment
Of tenderness

After the storm
After the rain

Gratitude

96

There is such a Tenderness
In this moment
That you can not
Not be here
This is where
I find You
And have no doubt
You are here

97

The Heart is pure
Just be immensely tender with yourself
Whatever anyone may think
Of what, who or where you are

98

Sometimes
It seems as
Even a droplet
May hurt the soft petal

99

Do not misunderstand!
Any of these words
Coming out of my pen

They are just words
That I need to hear

To tenderly comfort myself
And know

That I still
Can love someone

Even if
It is only myself

100

Blessing angel's touch
Delicate and silent

Drops of tenderness
Lightening billions of tiny sparkles

A moment
Softly blissful
Through the light breath
Of diamond tears

101

To you, precious rose lover
Who chose to disappear
From the mist of human's mind
Love is tender
Love is fragile
Love is what you are
Thank you for being

102

There is a mystery that some call love
Known as the deepest secret of the longing
Living a blind life
Through suffering and hatred
Caring and tenderness

Silent
The mystery is revealed
As the depth of this moment
When the mist becomes thicker
And no-one is talking

No silence between notes
But in the presence of the living heart
This mystery
Has Your name
And those thoughts
Carry your fragrant tenderness

103

If I sit
And look into the mirror that you are
I become Silence
From here
I hear words of love
Expression of deep Tenderness

104

I read in your smile the deep tenderness of your heart

105

I've never touched the wind
But it keeps on caressing my skin
Through a delicate and warm touch

106

Precious precious Tenderness of the Heart
That is alright
If You don't find me
That
Is Pure Tenderness...

107

Tenderness is so tender
But really
Don't look for it
Let it caress you

108

Feeling this deep call
Of Tenderness
Pulling me
In
That endless Silence

Silence

Peace

109

I draw from Your Silence
This boundless strength
Of Your Presence

110

The voice of Silence
Is the only Truth

111

O Sacred Moon!
Still and silent
Humble Presence
In the depth of the night

Here
Reflection of the most secret thought
In pure innocence

O precious Moon
Some One is hiding
In Your unshakable Presence

112

This mysterious
And intimate dance
Of human and divine
Is silently
Blissful

113

And suddenly
You became silent
Leaving the question
Without existence

114

In the Silence of the Heart
I find myself

115

Let Silence find its own way
And see the space left
When it comes
All those non-questions dissolving
In the present moment

116

I heard Your Silence
And I recognized My Voice

117

I wonder
If there is a whisper
Soft enough
Not to break
Your delicate Silence

118

At that moment
The Silence became unbearable for the mind
Totally splashed by the splendor of This
And I started to talk

119

If I could find words to tell You how I feel
I would stay Silent

120

Do you hear Silence?
It has nothing to say
Love is here

121

Have you ever listened to the song
Of the flower blooming?
The ladybird, yes

122

There is a secret
In the Universe
That is known
By the most silent hearts

123

From the deepest Silence
Emerges the purest Love

124

I love Your Silence
This world is full of words
Full of barriers and non-sense
Full of senses and hate
Full of misery and knowings
Full of me(s)
I love Your Silence
I love This Silence
This
Silence

125

Silence is my refuge
I see myself dreaming
Silence is my refuge
The Heart is patiently waiting
For the day to come
Silence is my refuge
I am at Peace
Alone

126

There are people
Who are able to see
The despair of the world
In a drop of Silence

127

Love knocked at my door
Several times today
I stayed silent
And kept Its warmth within

128

Drink until there's no thirst
Breathe until there's no air
Walk until there's no body
Love until there's no you
Until only Silence remains

129

There is a path with no road
Where Silence is met at any time of Truth
And it turns out to be my only Friend
Life starts again
After having gone
I am alone on this path

130

Back to Silence
I hear Your true voice

131

I can hear Your Call
It is clear
The pure Silent One

132

Tiny flower and shiny Moon
Let me send you
Some bright stars dust
Enjoy the soft melody
Of this silent song
Secretly lulling
Your lovely ears

Tiny flower and shiny Moon
Eyelids falling
Baby yawning
It's time to rest
And kiss your cheek
Holding that eternal breath

133

Silence allows to go deeper
And deeper
Always
Until Silence only
Is leading all

134

Silence is known
When Joy and Peace
Are One

135

Blessed is the one
Who can hear the sound of Silence
In a drop of this moment

136

O Silence!
I've been feeling You
Growing within
The whole day

Like a continuous chase
I saw myself trying to escape You
And You
Catching me back
To Your infinite place

So many times
Too many thoughts
For a sound or a word to be

O Silence !

I am so scared to fully melt in You
Feeling Your immense strength
Attracting me
In the depth
Of nothingness

O Silence!

Breathe in my fears
And all my thoughts
And become me

137

I fell in love with your Silence
There is nothing to say
Nothing to share
This Silence
Is so present
Giving birth to tears and laughter

I could fly away
Vanish in the sky
You would be here

Oh! Such humbling Presence
Where nothing can be grasped
All that is shared
Is self-collapsing
Into billions of inner stars

I kiss your Silence
Each time I close my mouth

138

Only thoughts can make love with each other
It is a restless night
Where the Prince belongs to the Princess

Like a candle in the wind
Nothing lights up the day
Till the wick is burnt

Oh those talks!
They are thoughts
Flowing like a river

Don't listen
But the sound
Of this moment

139

Even a song
Is Silence

140

For the One at Peace
Any word from this Universe
Is Silence

141

In the depth of Your Silence
I find nobody
And I call It mySelf

Stillness

142

The deep stillness of the Mountain
Patiently waits for the world to collapse
Making free
A melting Heart

See how Silence
Breaks through
Sometimes through bursting tears
Sometimes through tender care
Face this aloneness
Where the Mountain looks at You
And reflects the Truth
Of your inner strength
This Mountain is breathing You

143

The Stillness of this moment
Contains the sacredness of Your Heart

144

There is a place in my Heart
Where You are
Stillness of the moment

Waves of emotions
Are not as beautiful
As the depth of that place

Be still
And find that place
Where nobody
Is rejected

This is where You are
This is where I am
This is the only place
Where love is pure

145

There is a Mountain calling Your name!
Can you hear that call?
Stop wondering
And be still

Just...
Hear that Call
It is not a loud call
It is deep within
Always calling
From the root of Your Being

Just listen
To that Call
And know
There is a Mountain calling Your name

146

How not to be fully absorbed in Your unshakable
Stillness?
This glimpse of human fragility
Leads the mind to vanish in deep respect
Into Your Pure Being

To the one who doesn't see
I shout out
"Wake up !
And listen
To this silent song
Penetrating the core of Your own life!"

All...
All is contained
In Your Being

147

The Sky hasn't ever made any sound
It stands all
Still
Fly free

148

There is nothing to protect in me
The Being is pure
Stillness

149

Yes
I could have cried
But in the Stillness of the Heart
I heard the sound of the waves
Dying on the shore

150

Watching the blue sky
I remembered the stars
And realized
Night was here
Not before or after the day
But in the depth of this moment

151

Deep into the Earth
There is a Secret
I once came here
And left Your name
Now,
I walk on You

152

Let yourself
Dive deeper
In the Stillness
Of that moment

153

Do never trust a word
Do never trust a sound
But listen to the core of the unspoken
Hear the music of the living heart
And forget any moment that has ever existed
What remains
Has never betrayed anyone

154

Peace embraces all
And dissolves the appearance of
What love should be

155

Deep in the thick darkness
The only thing remaining
Is this breath of life

Soft, delicate and tender
Breath of life
Carrying that infinite Peace
Beyond any feeling of life or death

156

When I see That
I know
Something knows
And The Heart is at Peace
Om

157

Golden wings falling
From a green sky
In a perfect indifference
Of the walker passing by

158

The miracle is not to be still staring at the sky
The miracle is to be still within the storm

159

Do not care who
Do not care how
Do not care when
Be at peace
And forget yourself

160

Plant a seed of Peace in the Earth
And birds will spread their wings
Flying like angels
In your heart

161

See how fragile I am!
A single one of Your breaths
And I split
Into nameless sparkles of love

In the most desperate moment
Peace is always present
Namaste to the One

162

See the boat
Far away
Melting with the horizon
In the eternal setting sun
And remain where you are
Feet on Earth
Broken heart
Blessed
By the song
Of the quiet waves
Dying on the beach
After a loving day

O tender Peace
You never leave me
Infinite Gratitude
To You, the One
Who has never left

Light

Life

Sacredness

163

Love is the humility
Of the stars in the day
Light your candle
With the breath of Your Beloved
And see
The wavering tenderness
In the light of Faith
How often "I love You"
Closed the door of kindness
And still Light shines through
The door of humbleness
Forgive the healer
In Yourself
And be at Peace

164

Shadows, colors and light
Make the wonder
Of this ordinary moment

165

Rising straight from the sun
Splendor
Dawn

166

Behind the clouds
The Sun keeps on shining

167

See the colours beyond what appears to be..

168

See through each color of the rainbow
Dance with them all
And know
There must be a whole world
To make it real

169

I painted stars in the sky
So you'd remember me
In the darkness of the night

170

The view
Is always
Ever clear
From where we are

From That
Be still
And know

171

Drops of love
Falling on the wall
Are sparkles of light
From an endless universe
Dissolved by Grace

172

You may be blinded by the light
You see outside

Drink It
Fully
Absorb It
And let It dissolve You
Till no light

Be drunk from that Light
And let It be what you are

Don't stay blind
Become drunk

173

I turned the page form the book of my life this
morning
And I found a brand new blank page

The Sun touched my skin
And life started again
The new day has come

174

Life is a poem
You can write
On the surface of the sea
Sun is the pen
And makes the light shine through
No wave can change the words of the sun
As the light goes deep into the sea
And hides its secret
In the core of the Heart

175

I am both
The rainbow and the storm

My lightning is so profound
That it splits the Light
Into colors

176

If there was only light
Bees couldn't kiss the flowers
To make sweet honey

177

Love

Is the only word
Love said to me today
All the rest
Expands in space

From a single
Sparkle of love

178

I will dance in the sky
So brightly
That you'll remember your Self
In the deepest silent night

180

I saw flowers in the sky
And realized
My Heart was in bloom

181

Listening to the wind blowing
In the wild fields

Waiting for the sun to rise again
And shine through

The essence of life is calling
The Silence of Freedom

182

Thoughts fighting
Like the leaves in the autumn wind
How can they hurt the tree?
They are free to be
And to rest in Peace
Till they feed the soil
Through their devoted silent death

183

The Heart tore the sky apart today
I'm walking on dead branches
The roses have faded away
They need to be changed

184

As long as you are breathing
There is the flow of life unfolding

As long as you are thirsty
There is water to carry you home

As long as you are feeling
There is a touch that can wake you up

As long as you are sleeping
There is a new day to come

As long as you are still
Love is merging into You

As long as you are
I will be

185

How many times
Did I forget
To celebrate
The birth of the Sun
From the dawn?

186

Know that you are alive
At least in my Heart

187

The leaf is flying from the tree
The day has gone
Wind is stealing
The rest of life
From the veins of the leaf

The sun is low
Its light carries the nostalgia of the spring
The sap in the tree
Burns the warmth of the summer
Winter is coming

The leaf is resting
Under the fresh song
Of the pearls
Falling from the sky
Waiting for the snow
To melt with the ground

The sun is now sleeping
For the new day to come

188

As the river flows
Not a single drop of water
Is stuck anywhere
Dancing and singing
Nothing prevents the river
From merging with the sea

Such is
The river of life

189

I searched for You in the trees
I searched for You in the air
I searched for You in the field
In searched for You in space

I searched for You in my Heart
And I realized I was alive

190

You may love a flower
But what is most beautiful
Is to see the flower
Blossoming in love

191

You might be willing to cut the rose
Whose thorns hurt your heart

You may cut the rose
Whose beauty insults your mind

But you will never
Prevent the rose
From spreading its fragrance

And the rose disappears

192

Summer is coming
Though here
Where I am now
No season is passing

Summer is coming
And soon
It will be time
To meet the smell and sun
Of the summer

I miss winter
But know
Winter is coming too

193

Life does not exist without love

I may play endlessly with good and bad
I may think endlessly one has to reach the Truth
But love is found
In the stillness of the Heart
We all are the Heart
There is no fight worth
Living for
Peace is here
In the depth of this moment

Love gives life to life
And there is nothing but love

194

The beauty of the living waves can be enjoyed at peace
from the shore
As for the sailor, it is lived through acts and humility

195

Mother Earth is calling You home
Warmth, care and strength
Pure flow of life
Rivers, mountains and valleys
Torrents and Quakes
It is not a time for the flower to bloom

Mother Earth is calling You home

You can now rest
In Her womb
All is safe
And taken care of

You are at home

196

There is a Beauty in this moment
The knowing that
There is something beyond
What you see

197

She fell down
In a whirling dance
And called my name
"Look at me!
This is a death dance!
I am alive
And flying my last moment
My heart is singing now
I am alive!"

How graceful she was
In this moment
Happily whirling
Between life and death

Like a child playing joyfully
She made my heart wonder about
The absolute Beauty of this simple
Flower
Released from the tree

198

The real treasure
Is not the light that you see
But what is behind Your eyes

199

This
Is
So
Delicate
That
You
Can't
Touch
It
Without
Breaking
It

200

The Being is so pure
Stay in that place
My Friend
Nobody knows
The Being is so pure

201

Welcome this moment
The sacredness of this precious unique moment
Without knowing where the river flows

In the space of Your own Heart
This knowing
That You are loved
Beyond anything expressible

There is no wish for anything else
You know
The preciousness of this moment

202

Make
Love
With
The
Secret
Intimacy
Of
That
Moment

203

Take the most beautiful flower
Breathe her
Till no more
But this ephemeral fragrance alone

204

There is nothing that is not delicate and sacred when
seen from love

205

There is a secret life
In the Heart of the Mother
That was never born

206

You only enter the temple of Your Heart
Naked

207

I cried one single tear today

But that tear
Was coming from
A place
Of no sound

Carrying what can't
Ever be touched

The Dream

208

I dreamt
I was making the stars move
In the darkest night

209

I've always dreamt of love
Till I realized
I was the dream

210

See how grounded you are
Watching the Sky

211

I read the Sky
In Your single breath

212

The sky is flying under me
Am I dead ?

Can't see any reflection here
Am I dead ?

I don't mind who I am
I've disappeared…

Above the clouds
Resting under me

213

I am
Just a dream passing by
Neither alive
Nor dead
Just a dream passing by
Kissing the wind
Without having ever existed

214

Back in time
I watched the sun setting
Afraid of its disappearance

Then I woke up
And saw
The sunset
Was the Blessing
Of that moment

215

The day I forget to hear the bird singing
Recall me that I am dead

216

The words of the poet
Are the stars of His Soul

217

I saw a butterfly flying
And I forgot I had a lover

218

When you reach your heart
Your life becomes a poem
And your words are notes
Singing the song
Of the wild flowers

219

The sky walks
Under your feet

220

The soul of the poet can't be stolen anymore
It has already flown away

221

Love is so mysterious
A dance through emotions
Without any known dancer

Just the dance

Its rhythm is
The lightness of the thought

There is no dancer
But the dance

Just allow yourself to dance
And let go the dancer
For this single moment

And that moment
Becomes eternal

222

Waves of thoughts
Are bathed
In the sky

The Dream

223

Meet me at the rainbow's end
Where there is no sea
Nor sky
Just the illusion of colors
Floating in the clouds
This is where I am

224

The only dream I had
Is that You were leaving

225

She held Her name for a second
In the echoing Silence of Her breath
Clouds became the nest
Of Her purest dream

226

There is a myth
That one has to die to live

There is a myth
That one has to be kinder

There is a myth
That one can always be happy

There is a myth
That life can be better

There is a myth
That one can change the world

There is a myth
That one can heal

There is a myth
That love has to be found

There is a myth
That one can understand

There is a myth
That there is something beyond That

The Dream

There is a myth
That one can realize the Truth

A myth known by someone

And no-one to know it

227

Try to catch the wind
And you'll be exhausted
You'll miss all the beauty
In the stillness of the moment
You'll miss its caress in your hair
You'll miss its softness on the grass
You'll miss the shiver of its breath

Try to lift the sky
And you'll be exhausted
You'll miss the space
In the light of the place
You'll miss its purity
You'll miss its color
You'll miss its infinity

Flow with the wind
Till its last breath
Fly in the sky
Till no more earth

228

I
See
Such
A deep
Desire
In
This emptiness
Of
Desire
That
The desire
Has
Become
Emptiness
Itself

229

The Heart is crying here
My eyes are dry
But the leaves are happy
To drink
The tears of the sky

Surrender

230

She let go
She let go of her pride
Of being the one perfect
Fearless and strong
Committed to the wellbeing of others before all

She allowed the flow of tears
Releasing that space
Where no one could enter

Through that moment of Grace
Flowers started to blossom
And the blessing "I love You"
Made her free
And empty

231

I let go of your name
And I found myself

232

To the peaceful One, I surrender my worries
To the compassionate One, I surrender my pain
To the joyful One, I surrender my sorrow
To the One in love, I surrender my Self

233

A desperate longing
For That that can never be touched
That desperation
Takes root
In the depth of Faith
And gives birth to the greatest
Surrender

234

I searched for You
Many different ways to express It
But none were restful

I keep on being
While knowing
That there is only You

235

There is no need to die from anything
But to watch the dance in Silence

This moment
Is the only thing
Which can bring You
To itself

Surrender

236

The unconditional love
That You seek
Is already
Here

237

Knowing Your unshakable Presence
Allows me
To be human

238

Go back to yourself
Let the world disappear
In the core of Your Heart

The softness of this breath
Will heal your pain

How blessed You are
To know the Heart

239

There is no way
But to let the river flow
By itself

Knowing
There is no-one
To hold the river

From there
The river keeps on flowing
Without destination

240

For the love of love
I meet you in the night
And wish upon stars

For the love of love
I see your smile
In the white rose in bloom

For the love of love
I cry with your tears
When I can't dry your cheeks

For the love of love
I give up having you
At my side hugging me

For the love of love
I wait for you
Till I know you are here

For the love of love
I look at the sky everyday
And lose myself in its sun

For the love of love
I forget your name

Surrender

And recognize your voice
In the silent butterfly

For the love of love
I surrender my name
For you to find me
In the air that you breathe

241

That is already happening
As if the dance has never ceased
And is embracing all
That is

Getting drunk in the whirling of love
There is no dancer here
There is no dancer here

Just dance
Embracing all
From the bottomless core
To the end of space

242

How often I cross the desert
Alone
Without any drink to quench my thirst
Until the moment I know
This desert walk
Is the most intimate communion
With myself

243

I like to write
Not because there is a need to talk
But a need to make words free

244

Fly away butterfly !
Fly away!
You'll never disappear
As you are always here
In that endless Heart!

Know you've already transformed
Into any single touch of Beauty
That life spreads on my path

Fly away butterfly!
Don't search for me!
I am the air holding your wings!

245

Be free like a bird
Fly for me!

246

Be free like a bird sweet heart
Be free
Fly on the moon
And flow with the wind
Across oceans
Dancing your freedom
On the top of the waves
Fly angel
Fly
You are freedom

Aloneness

247

When I saw the clouds crying
I knew that today
I would meet You in the rain
I walked down the path
And I smiled to the tiny drops here
Knowing that the sun
Would dry them all
In a glimpse of His Presence
I enjoy now the freshness of the clear and silent air
After the blessing rain

248

You see strength in me, remember I am fragility
You see fragility in me, remember I am strength

You see light in me, remember I am darkness
You see darkness in me, remember I am light

You see doubt in me, remember I am knowledge
You see knowledge in me, remember I am doubt

You see kindness in me, remember I am harshness
You see harshness in me, remember I am kindness

You see Faith in me, remember I don't know anything
You see absence of knowing in me, remember I am Faith

You see tenderness in me, remember I am roughness
You see roughness in me, remember I am tenderness

You see joy in me, remember I am sadness
You see sadness in me, remember I am joy

You see happiness in me, remember I am despair
You see despair in me, remember I am happiness

You see yourself in me, remember I am You
You see myself in you, remember You are me

You see love in me, remember You are love

249

You are
Your own
Source
Of infinite Love

The One
You think
You have to find

Is the One
Who is
Within you

You already
Know
Yourself
So deeply
That you have
Become
It

250

I met a flower on the path
And I rested by its side

In the silence of the trembling wind
It started to talk

"Why do you cry little girl?
There are no more clouds in the sky
I don't know the sea and don't have any friends
And yet, I have blossomed
My roots are deep as the mystery of Mother Earth
My heart flows through the sap watered by the rain
My shiny colors are only reflections of the bright sun
I am alive
I see You
And I hear You
I see Your sadness
And though I am alive
I am alone
And I shine brightly
For a single moment of my life
Spent by Your side"

251

The night is coming

I need a walk
I need some fresh air

I need a walk
And to put my feet on the earth

Guessing the bees are dancing
Saying goodnight
And blessing the day

Hearing the first timid crickets
Singing their love songs
And giving birth to the night

The last bird saying goodbye
The first star shining in the clear sky

I need a walk

The wind softly caressing my hair
And blowing the last thoughts of the day

I need a walk

I am alone
In the mountain

252

I thought I was walking with you on that path
Suddenly, I met only Silence
I looked backward
You had disappeared
I had always been walking alone

253

He left her on the shore
Naked

Anchored in Grace
The reed flew away
And reached
The unknown ocean

254

Make love with your own thoughts

255

Each time You gave me birth
You took my life back
Now...
I do not care to die or live
Just...
Don't give me anything anymore
Let me be
I am
Alone

256

Your loneliness is mine
Your Aloneness, Beauty

257

The Heart keeps on melting
Alone
In the sea
Of love

258

Breathtaking beauty of the human Heart
This space between sparkles and emptiness

Sacred and bright Presence
Bursting out of pain
In this majestic surrender
To the human Being

This Heart
Is the only thing I had
Now, it is Yours

259

The treasure
Is
In the Garden of Your Heart

260

There is nothing which can change
The deep Silence
Of Your Heart

261

There is no absence
In the Heart
But only
That infinite Presence
That You are

262

The Heart is bleeding love
Tell me my friend
Who is here?

263

The bridge is the Heart
And we are all
Walking in

264

Thoughts swing in the air
Between good and bad
Life and death
Tiny and immense
Here and beyond

Still
Watching them
A rainbow appears
That no-one can touch

The heart
Keeps the memory
Of the moment
That has never existed

265

The Heart is singing at the crossroad
Of so many thoughts
No idea at all which one is happy
The song is anchored
In the space of your heart

266

Wisdom and humility
Come from heart break
Let the tears flow
Till you become
The river itself

267

The Sky knows
The secret of your heart
Before you do

268

He took my heart
And I never came back

This book is, and always was, an offering from the Heart. I see it as a gift received from life. There has never been any personal will to write and publish such a book, but it happened.

Therefore, there is no aim to make any profit from it and all the money earned from its sales will be used to send picture-books to kids in countries where they cannot afford to buy books for their pleasure.

I am deeply grateful for this journey where each step is an opening to new possibilities.

Thank you for your love.

Hélène Avérous

www.heleneaverous.com

www.ingramcontent.com/pod-product-compliance
Lightning Source LLC
Chambersburg PA
CBHW031848090426
42741CB00005B/400

* 9 7 8 9 8 1 0 7 9 0 7 2 1 *